HUMOROUS ART SONGS
FOR SOLO VOICE

Compiled and Edited by
Barbara Meister

Ed. 3456

G. SCHIRMER, Inc.

DISTRIBUTED BY

HAL•LEONARD®
CORPORATION
7777 W. BLUEMOUND RD. P.O. BOX 13819 MILWAUKEE, WI 53213

CONTENTS

PREFACE

The essence of an art song, whether comic, tragic, or in between, is the relationship of the words to the music. Unlike an operatic aria, whose appeal may lie in vocal pyrotechnics or a folk song whose unsophisticated verses are usually set to the simplest chords, an art song, especially if it is post-Schubertian, will attempt to utilize words and music as equal partners to convey the mood and meaning of the text.

If a composer chooses an amusing poem and simply sets it so that the words can be understood without excessively high notes or obfuscating fioratura, the effect of the song will certainly be comic. But the best humorous art songs are those in which the music itself is part of the fun. The deliberate bumbling in the postlude of Hugo Wolf's "Wie lange schon war immer mein Verlangen," and the exaggerated formality of the cadences in Mussorgsky's "The Classicist," are delightful little musical jokes which aid and abet or, as in the Wolf, even replace—the humor of the words.

The following brief descriptions of the songs in this collection are intended to help singers and accompanists in their efforts to entertain and amuse audiences with this relatively neglected category of vocal repertoire.

B.M.

NOTES

1. Why should'st thou swear I am forsworn   by Charles I (1600-1649)

Charles I, King of England from 1625 to 1649, is probably best remembered for losing his head, for the trial and execution which ended his reign was an unprecedented event in British history. Ruling autocratically, arbitrarily, and for long periods of time without the aid of Parliament, Charles I is not remembered for his love of the arts. Nevertheless he was an ardent admirer of Shakespeare, a sophisticated and knowledgeable art collector, and a musician of some talent. This song by the unfortunate monarch, who was, by all contemporary accounts, far too uxorious to have indulged in the kind of dalliance suggested by its text, exhibits a sly and subtle sense of humor.

2. The Cunning Constable   by Richard Leveridge (1670-1758), text by Henry Bold

3. Rumpled, Tumbled and Jumbled   by authors unknown

Judging from the many collections featuring comic songs published in England in the seventeenth and eighteenth centuries, *Wit's Recreations* (1640), *Wit's Interpreter* (1655), *Choyce Drollery* (1656), *Merry Drollery* (1661), *Oxford Drollery* (1671) etc., musical humor was very much in vogue in Elizabethan and post-Elizabethan times. In 1719 Thomas D'Urfey began a six-volume series entitled *Wit and Mirth, or Pills to Purge Melancholy* which included 1,144 songs and poems of a comic nature. "The Cunning Constable" and "Rumpled, Tumbled and Jumbled" are from this amusing and often highly ribald collection.

Written in 1685 by Henry Bold (words) and Richard Leveridge (music), "The Cunning Constable" was inspired by the many men who hid or ran away to escape impressment into the British army by the constable responsible for rounding them up. Depending on one's audience, one might or might not want to point out the somewhat raw pun in the title!

The creators of "Rumpled, Tumbled and Jumbled" are uncredited by Mr. D'Urfey, who may have composed the song himself. Whoever did write the verses shows a fine disrespect for such authority figures as the judge and the parson.

4. Amos, Amas, I Love a Lass   by Samuel Arnold (1740-1802)

Samuel Arnold, a most extraordinary musician, lived in London from 1740 to 1802. Renowned as a composer, conductor, organist, scholar, and impresario, Dr. Arnold produced almost one hundred stage pieces in which music was an integral ingredient. Sometimes he composed original scores for them, but often he used pastiches of the music of Bach, Galuppi, Handel, and others. This little ditty, a charming English counterpart to the Mussorgsky "Seminarist" (obviously the study of Latin was a problem of international scope in the eighteenth and nineteenth centuries), was introduced in a musical entitled *The Agreeable Surprise* first performed at the Haymarket Theatre on September 3, 1781.

5. Warnung   by W.A. Mozart (1756-1791)

Mozart's melodic inventiveness is a given in the world of music. His thematic lines, be they written for instruments or the human voice, sing with an inevitable rightness that renders them appealing to the most cultivated as well as the most naive listener. Yet this master of opera, who composed many of the greatest arias in the entire repertoire, wrote remarkably few songs for solo voice. Even within this small output—thirty-six pieces for voice and piano—many are slight efforts, not really representative of Mozart's great lyric genius. There are, of course, exceptions, notably "Das Veilchen," "Abendempfindung," and "Als Louise die Briete." Not in this exalted league, but delightful and charming nevertheless, is the slightly naughty "Warnung" (A Warning), in which fathers are admonished to keep their daughters safely at home. The song has the lilting grace of many a soubrette aria by the incomparable Wolfgang Amadeus.

6. Der Kuss
by L. van Beethoven (1770-1827)

The scowling face revealed in most busts and portraits of Ludwig van Beethoven ill prepares the music lover for the zesty, earthy, often boisterous humor in much of his music. From the teasing introduction to the last movement of the *First Symphony,* the mock fury in the piano Rondo (1823), and the parodistic close of the *Variations on a Theme by Count Waldstein* for piano four-hands (1792), Beethoven is alternately puckish, playful, and satirical. Two of his songs, "The Flea" and "The Kiss" (Opp. 75, No. 3 and 128 respectively), show him at his wittiest. "The Flea," based on the famous Goethe poem (its official title is "Aus Goethe's Faust") and also set felicitously by Mussorgsky and Berlioz, is a brilliant political satire. "The Kiss" is a wry comment on demure young maidens.

7. Vergebliches Ständchen
by J. Brahms (1833-1897)

As dour in reputation as his idol Beethoven, Johannes Brahms was a lonely bachelor whose ambiguous platonic attachment to Clara Schumann was fraught with Oedipal overtones. Some of his music is ponderous and dark, weighted with the responsibility of being Beethoven's musical heir. But there are many wonderful exceptions, compositions radiating high spirits and infectious rhythms—the Hungarian Dances, the Opus 39 Waltzes, the "Zigeunerlieder" Opus 103, the "Liebeslieder Waltzes," to name a few.

Equally strong evidence of his love for lighthearted music are songs such as "Vergebliches Ständchen" (A Futile Serenade), Op. 84, No. 4, in which the young maiden saucily dismisses her maladroit suitor. It is the solo singer's task to portray both parties in this abortive romantic interlude.

8. Wie lange schon war immer mein Verlangen
by Hugo Wolf (1860-1903)

9. Ich liess mir sagen
(Italienisches Lieberbuch)

There is virtually no human emotion—whether it is grief, joy, lust, religious piety, despair, contentment, pride, greed or erotic ecstasy—that does not find expression in the Liederbücher (Song Books) of Hugo Wolf. Since humor is part of the human experience, it is also part of Wolf's superb song catalogue, and at least a dozen fine examples, ranging from the broadest jocularity to the most subtle irony, may be found among the Mörike, Italienische, and Eichendorff collections. The two chosen for inclusion here, "How Often Have I Prayed" (for a musician for a husband—strange prayer!) and "I Was Informed," are fairly representative. The humor of the first is very broad: Tonio is so lovesick that he is pining away, eating no more than seven sausages and seven loaves for every one of his molars. (The mock-serious trills in the accompaniment help set the tongue-in-cheek mood.) The second song is much more subtle, beginning with what seems like genuine pathos and depending on a halting, limping, deliberately clumsy rendering of the piano postlude for its punch line. The fiddler whom the maiden finally captures is obviously a pretty poor one, as one can tell from the misplaced accents and long, stumbling trill at the end, all carefully indicated by the composer.

10. **Des Antonius von Padua Fischpredigt**   by Gustav Mahler (1860-1911)
    (Lieder aus Des Knaben Wunderhorn)

11. **Starke Einbildungskraft**
    (Lieder und Gesänge aus der Jugendzeit)

The music of Gustav Mahler, long in partial eclipse, has finally begun to receive the attention it merits. His remarkable symphonies, which often incorporate voice in the tradition of Beethoven's Ninth, are encountered more and more frequently, as his admirers grow in number and enthusiasm. There has been a concomitant rise in interest in Mahler's songs, those with orchestral settings as well as those with piano accompaniment. Since the best known of these songs, *Lieder eines fahrenden Gesellen* (Songs of the Wayfarer) and *Kindertotenlieder* (Songs on the Death of Children) are more than a little lugubrious, singers seldom think of Mahler as a source of humor. Nevertheless there are several songs, including the two in this collection, that are both charming and amusing. The first, "Saint Anthony Preaches to the Fishes," is satirical in its mock seriousness. Its poem, like that of the other Mahler song presented here, is taken from the anthology of sixteenth-, seventeenth-, and eighteenth-century German poetry known as *Des Knaben Wunderhorn*, "The Youth's Magic Horn." Although the piano accompaniment can never duplicate the brilliance of the original orchestral score, some of the flavor of its bells and muted cymbals is suggested by frequent grace notes. "Strong Imagination" proves that even in 1882, when Mahler wrote this delightfully rueful vignette, women often had to be the more earthy agressors in romantic situations.

12. **J'aime l'amour**   by Georges Bizet (1838-1875)

Bizet's "Carmen" is certainly among the five or six most popular operas ever written, yet when it was first produced (1875) it was such a critical failure that its composer went into a decline from which he never recovered, dying a few months later at the age of thirty-seven. Other composers might have weathered the blasts of the critics but Bizet already suffered from low self-esteem, deeming his few dozen songs unworthy of serious attention. While perhaps not a masterpiece, "I Love Love" charms us with its lilting melody, its dancing rhythm, and its Gallic expression of the when-I'm-not-near-the-girl-I-love-I-love-the-girl-I'm-near syndrome!

13. **Ballade des gros dindons**   by Emmanuel Chabrier (1841-1894)

14. **Villanelle des petits canards**

Animals' antics are always amusing, and the more anthropomorphic their behavior, the more humorous they appear to us. Several animal songs are included here, and many others may be found, especially in the French repertoire (Poulenc's "Le Bestiaire" which has songs about camels, goats, and fish; Ravel's "Histoires naturelles" which treats crickets, peacocks, and swans among others; Milhaud's "Les Quatre petits lions", etc.). These two by Chabrier, "The Ballad of the Fat Turkeys" and the "Villanelle of the Little Ducks," are part of a set which also describes pink pigs and green grasshoppers, but they are often programmed separately. Incidentally, the author of the poem which serves as text for "Les Gros Dindons" is Edmond Rostand, who is far more famous for his brilliant play "Cyrano de Bergerac." Chabrier's ducks are gay little fellows who become quite romantic (the word "amoureux" in the last verse should be exaggeratedly expressive, making the effect of a very nasal rendering of "nasillards" in the next measure all the more comic). The turkeys, in the other song, must be made to strut about as pompously as possible.

15. The Classicist   by Modeste Mussorgsky (1839-1881)

16. The Seminarist

Considering the rough treatment often given to composers by conservative critics, it is not surprising to find several witty counterattacks in the comic art-song literature. Two are included in this collection—Charles Ives's "The One Way" and Mussorgsky's "The Classicist." "The Classicist" is specifically dedicated to a fierce enemy of the new Russian school, A. S. Faminitsyn, a Petrograd Professor who translated the classics into a dry, lifeless formula which he expected all composers to follow. The song ends with a devastatingly correct final cadence. "The Seminarist" describes a Latin student who cannot keep his mind on conjugations and declensions when his teacher's nubile daughter passes by.

17. If You've Only Got a Moustache   by Stephen Foster (1826-1864)

18. My Wife is a Most Knowing Woman

To some classical purists, the piano rags of Scott Joplin or the songs of Stephen Foster are anathema. In truth, they were conceived as popular entertainment, but the unerring good taste of their composers make them welcome as lighter-weight encores or concluding numbers. "If You've Only Got a Moustache" and "My Wife is a Most Knowing Woman" are wonderfully evocative of the era in which they were written (1863-64), a time when a splendid handle-bar moustache was a definite aid to romance and when women ruled only from behind the scene.

19. The One Way   by Charles Ives (1874-1954)

Ives wrote many of his own texts, including the sardonic "The One Way," a put-down of imitative composers and the listeners and critics who prefer them. Scattered among the insipid tonic triads and V-1 cadences are several wicked little Ivesian dissonances (under "bring a smile," in the accompaniment before "Now a softer cadence," under "now we change the key," etc.) to reinforce the point.

20. Promiscuity   by Samuel Barber (1910-1981)

21. Church Bell at Night

These two brief vignettes from Samuel Barber's ten-song cycle *Hermit Songs,* Op. 29, give a rather cynical view of female morality. The humor in the latter song is underscored by the clangerous cacophony Barber attributes to the "sweet little bell." The texts of the cycle, composed in 1953, are translations from anonymous Irish poems of the eighth through the thirteenth centuries.

22. A Fine Line   by Seymour Barab (1921-   )

The art song repertoire abounds in. declarations of undying love. It is refreshing to find an antidote for the usual overdose of sentimentality—Barab's caustic "A Fine Line," which ends "to love you is pleasant enough, but oh, it's delicious to hate you"! Thomas Moore's wry poem is tongue-in-cheek, deceptively sweet and lyrical, inviting the singer to set up the punch line by sounding as loving as possible until the very last phrase.

Why Should'st Thou Swear
I Am Forsworn

Charles I

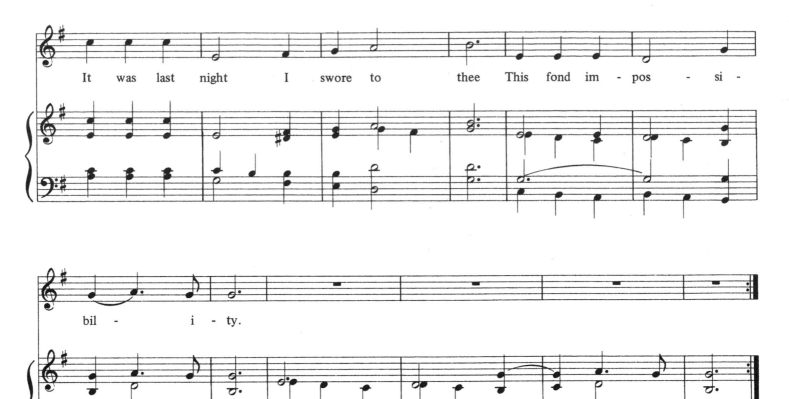

It was last night I swore to thee This fond im - pos - si - bil - i - ty.

2. Have I not lov'd thee much and long,
   A tedious twelve hours' space!
   I should all other beauties wrong
   And rob thee of a new embrace,
   Should I still dote upon thy face.

3. Not that all joys in thy brown hair
   By others may be found;
   But I will search the dark, the fair,
   Like skilful min'ralists that found
   Their treasures in unploughed ground.

The Cunning Constable

Henry Bold

Richard Leveridge

2.   Ho, who's at home? Lo, here am I!
Good morrow neighbour! Welcome, Sir!
Where's your husband? Why, truly,
He's gone abroad, a journey far.
Do you not know when he comes back?—
(See how these cowards fly for life!)—
The king for soldiers must not lack:
If I miss the man, I'll take the wife!

3.   Show me by what authority
You do it - pray, Sir, let me know!
It is sufficient for to see
The warrant hangs in the bag below.
Then pull it out - if it be strong,
With you I will not stand at strife!
My warrant is as broad as long:
If I miss the man, I'll press the wife!

4. Now you have pressed me, and are gone,
Please you but let me know your name,
That when my husband he comes home
I may declare to him the same.
My name is Captain *Ward,* I say—
I ne'er feared man in all my life.
The king for soldiers must not stay:
Missing the man, I'll press the wife!

Rumpled, Tumbled and Jumbled

Anonymous

6

Add at end of first and last verses only

Then rose and went from me as soon as he'd done!

If he be not ham - pered for serv - ing me so, May I be worse

½CII

rump - led, Worse tum - bled and jum - bled, Wher - ev - er, wher - ev - er I go!

2 Before an old justice I summoned the spark:
And how do you think I was served by his clerk?
He pulled out his inkhorn, and asked me his fee:
You now shall relate the whole business, quoth he!
He pressed me etc.

3 The justice then came: though grave was his look,
Seemed to wish I would kiss him, instead of The Book!
He whispered his clerk then, and, leaving the place,
I was had to his chamber to open my case!
He pressed me etc.

4 I went to our parson to make my complaint:
He looked like a *Bacchus*, but preached like a saint.
He said we should soberly nature refresh,
Then nine times he urged me to humble the flesh!
He pressed me, I stumbled,
He pushed me, I tumbled,
He kissed me, I grumbled,
But still he kissed on,
Then rose and went from me as soon as he'd done!
If he be not hampered for serving me so,
May I be worse rumpled,
Worse tumbled and jumbled,
Wherever, wherever I go!

Amo, Amas, I Love a Lass

Samuel Arnold

gen - der. Ro - rum Co - rum sunt di - vo - rum, Ha - rum

sca - rum di - vo; Tag rag mer-ry der-ry, per- i -wig and hat- band,

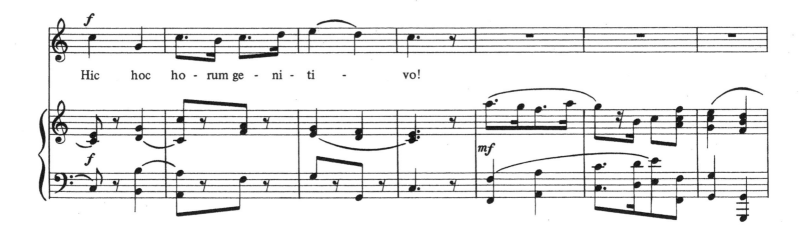

Hic hoc ho- rum ge - ni - ti - vo!

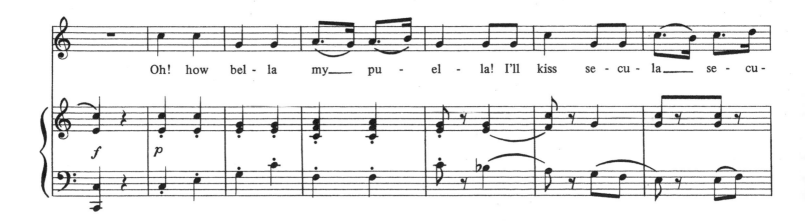

Oh! how bel - la my___ pu - el - la! I'll kiss se - cu - la___ se - cu-

lo - rum; If I've luck, sir, she's my___ ux - or, O dies ___

be - ne - dic - to - rum! Ro - rum Co - rum sunt di - vo - rum, Ha - rum

sca - rum di - vo; Tag rag mer - ry der - ry, per - i - wig and hat - band,

Hic hoc ho - rum ge - ni - ti - vo!

A Warning
(Warnung)

Wolfgang Amadeus Mozart

Män - ner su - chen stets zu na - schen,
Ev' - ry man is fond of dain - ties

lässt _____ man sie al - lein, _____ lässt _____ man sie al - lein; _____
If _____ he get his way, _____ if _____ he get his way; _____

leicht _____ sind Mad - chen zu er - ha - schen, weiss _____ man sie zu ü - ber
Though _____ he court a maid he'll leave her, Prove _____ him - self a base de -

ra - schen, weiss man sie zu ü-ber-ra-schen. Soll das
ceiv - er, prove him-self a base de-ceiv-er. Can you

zu ver-wun-dern___ sein, Soll das zu ver-wun-dern___ sein? Mäd-chen
great-ly won-der,___ pray? Can you great-ly won-der,___ pray? Fair and

ha - ben fri - sches Blut,___ und das Na - schen schmeckt so gut,___
fresh, and slim of waist,___ Maids are vast-ly to his taste:___

und das Na schen schmeckt so___ gut, und das___ Na schen schmeckt so___
maids are___ vast-ly___ to his___ taste, maids are___ vast-ly___ to his___

(più forte)

gut, schmecht so gut, schmecht so gut!
taste, to his taste, to his taste!

Doch das Na-schend vor dem' Es - sen nimmt___ den Ap-pe - tit,___
Eat -ing sweets be-fore one's meal - time spoils ___ the ap-pe - tite, ___

nimmt___ den Ap-pe - tit. ___ Man - che kam, die das ver-ges - sen, um den
spoils ___ the ap-pe - tite. ___ Ma - ny a maid through fick- le lov - er, Los - es

Schatz, den sie be - ses - sen, und um ih - ren Lieb - sten___ mit, und um
what she'll ne'er re - cov - er, Of this fact for- get - ful ___ quite, of this

ih - ren Lieb - sten mit. Va - ter lasst's euch's War - nung sein, sperrt die
fact for - get - ful quite. Fa - thers all, take heed of this: Keep her

Zu - cker - plätz - chen ein, sperrt die Zu - cker - plätz - chen
close each pret - ty miss. Keep her close each pret - ty

ein! Va - ter
miss! Fa - thers,

lasst euch's War - nung sein, sperrt die Zu - cker - plätz - chen
take good heed of this: keep her close, each pret - ty

14

The Kiss
(Der Kuss)

C.F. Weisse

Ludwig Van Beethoven, Op. 128

poco ritard   _a tempo_

es sei ver - geb - ne Müh, ver - geb - ne___ Müh, es sei ver -
And if I tried to kiss her 'twould be a ___ fright, And if I

geb - ne, ver geb-ne Müh.   Ich wagt es doch, und kuss-te sie, und küss-te
tried to kiss 'twould be a fright.   But I ig - nored the words she said And kissed her

sie, trotz ih - rer Ge - gen - wehr, trotz ih - rer___ Ge - gen-wehr.
on her ros - y li - ps in - stead, On her___ ros-y lips_____ in - stead.

Poco Adagio   _Tempo I_ **f**

Und schrie sie___ nicht?   Ja
And did she___ cry?   Yes,

wohl, sie schrie,   sie schrie;   doch,   doch, doch lan- ge hin- ter-
yes, she cried,   she cried;   yes,   yes, la - ter, much la -

(laughing)
fz
f
sf p

her,   doch,   ja doch!, doch lan- ge hin- ter- her, sie schrie,___ doch___
ter,   yes,   la - ter, much la - ter she   cried, she cried___ much___

cresc.
cresc.

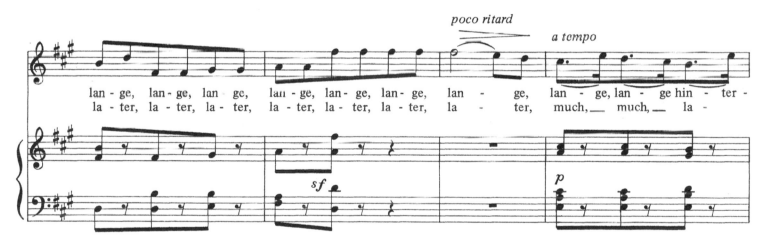

lan - ge, lan - ge, lan ge,   lan - ge, lan - ge, lan - ge, lan - ge, lan - ge, lan - ge hin - ter-
la - ter, la - ter, la - ter,   la - ter, la - ter, la - ter, la - ter, much,___ much,___ la -

poco ritard
a tempo
sf
p

her,   hin - ter- her, ja lan- ge, lan   - ge hin - ter- her.
ter,   la - ter,___ much__ la - ter, la - ter.

short
mf
cresc.
f

A Rustic Serenade
(Vergebliches Ständchen)

From the Folklore of the Lower Rhineland
English text by B.M.

Johannes Brahms, Op. 84, No. 4

She:

Mein'_ Tür_ ist ver - schlos - sen, ich lass'_ dich nicht
My_ door is lock'd, it's stay - ing lock'd, I will not let you

ein, ich lass'_ dich nicht ein;
in, I will not let you in;

Mut - ter, die rät mir klug, wärst du her - ein mit _ Fug, wär's mit mir vor -
Moth - er gives good ad - vice, She's told me more than _ twice, It would be a

bei, wär's mit mir, wär's mit mir, wärs mit mir _ vor - bei!
sin, it would be, it would be, it would be _ a sin.

20

He:
So_ kalt_ ist die Nacht,_ so ei - sig der
The_ night is dark, The air is chill, The i-cy wind blows

Wind,
wild,
so ei - sig der Wind,
The i - cy wind blows wild.

dass mir das Herz er - friert, mein' Lieb' er - lö - schen_ wird öff - ne mir, mein Kind,
My heart can - not be_ bold If it is fro - zen with cold. Let me in, my child,

Lebhafter (livelier)

öff - ne mir, öff - me mir, öff - ne mir, mein Kind!
Let me in, Let me in, Let me in,_ my child.

21

She:

Lö - schet dein' Lieb, lass sie, lö - schen nur, lass sie
If your love's cold let it per - ish, let it reach an end, Let your

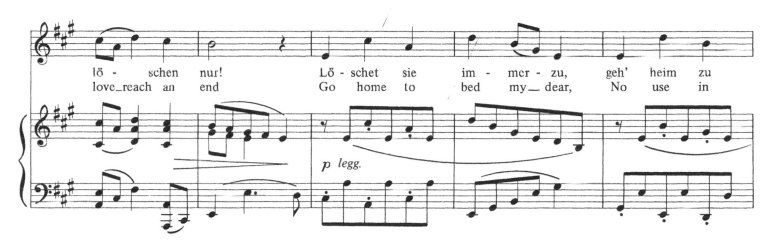

lö - schen nur! Lö - schet sie im - mer - zu, geh' heim zu
love reach an end Go home to bed my dear, No use in

Bett, zur Ruh', gu - te Nacht, mein Knab', gu - te Nacht, gu - te Nacht,
wait - ing here. Good night my friend, good night, good night,

gu - te Nacht, mein Knab'!
good night, my friend.

How Often Have I Prayed
(Wie lange schon war immer mein Verlangen)

from *Italienisches Liederbuch*
Paul Heyse

Hugo Wolf

Sehr langsam und nicht ohne Humor ♩ = 40
(always slow and not without humor)

gefühlvoll (tenderly)

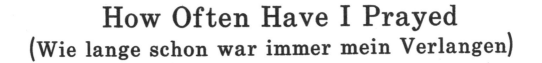

Wie
How

lan - ge schon war im - mer mein Ver - lan - gen: ach,
of - ten have I prayed in fer - vent mood that

wä - re doch ein Mu - si - kus mir gut!
a mu - si - cian might my true love be.

Nun ___ liess der Herr, mich ___ mei - nen Wunsch er -
Now ___ gra - cious Heav'n, in ___ ver - y flesh and

lan - gen und schickt mir ei - nen, ___ ganz wie Milch ___ und
blood, ___ the man of my de - sire ___ has sent ___ to

Blut.
me.

Da kommt er e - ben
See here he comes a -

her mit ___ sanf - ter Mie - ne, und
long with ___ gent - le looks ___ and

senkt den Kopf und spielt die Vi - o -
bows his head and plays the vi - o -

li - ne.
lin. _____

recht zaghaft und schwankend (quite emphatic and moving)

immer leise (always softer)

zögernd (hold back)

(long trill)
tr

I Was Informed

(Ich liess mir sagen)

from *Italienisches Liederbuch*

Paul Heyse

Hugo Wolf

Ich liess mir sa - gen und mir ward er - zählt,
I was in - for - med and I grieved to hear,

der schö - ne To - ni hung - re sich zu To - de;
That my dear To - ni is of hun - ger dy - ing;

seit ihn so ü - ber - aus die Lie - be quält
For since the pangs of love are so se - vere

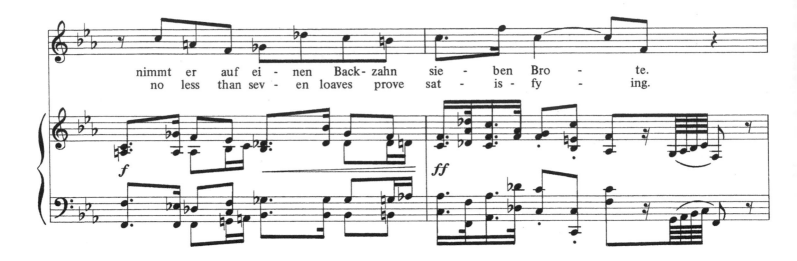

nimmt er auf ei - nen Back - zahn sie - ben Bro - te.
no less than sev - en loaves prove sat - is - fy - ing.

Nach Tisch, _____ da - mit er die Ver - dau - ung stählt,
and then, _____ to strength - en his di - ges - tive pow'r,

ver - speist er ei - ne Wurst und sie - ben Bro - te,
a sau - sage, too, he'll eat with - in the hour, ___

und lin - dert nicht To - ni - na sei - ne Pein,
So if To - ni - na does not ease his pain,

bricht näch - stens Hun - gers - not und Teu - rung ein.
of fa - mine in the land we'll soon com - plain.

Anthony of Padua Preaches to the Fish
(Des Antonius von Padua Fischpredigt)

from *Lieder aus Knaben Wunderhorn (1888)*
Very freely translated by B.M.

Gustav Mahler

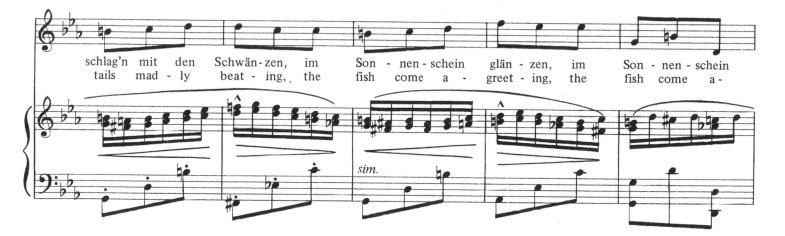

schlag'n mit den Schwän-zen, im Son-nen-schein glän-zen, im Son-nen-schein
tails mad-ly beat-ing, the fish come a-greet-ing, the fish come a-

Son-nen-schein glän-zen, sie glän-zen, sie glän-zen, glän-zen!
greet-ing, the fish come a-greet-ing, a-greet-ing, greet-ing!

Die Karp-fen mit Ro-gen seind all hier-her
The carp filled with egg roe, Their mouths form a

zo-gen; hab'n d'Mäu-ler auf ris-en sich Zu hör'ns-be-flis-sen.
round "O," Each ea-ger ear reach-es To hear what he preach-es.

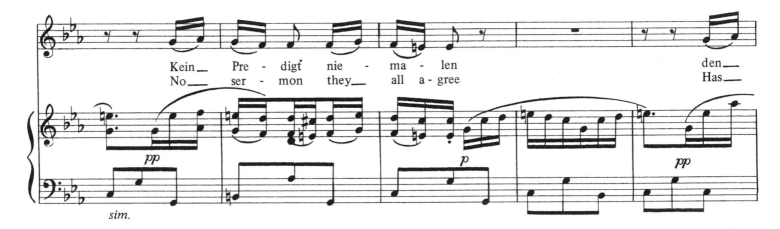

Kein__ Pre - digt_ nie - ma - len den__
No__ ser - mon they__ all a - gree Has__

sim.

Fi - schen so__ g'fal - len!
pleased_them so__ swim-ming-ly. *(with humor)*

Spitz - go - sche - te Hech - te, die im - mer - zu fech - ten, sind

Pike thin lipped with spite___ Are read - y to___ fight,___ Have

ei - lends her schwom - men, zu hö - ren den From - men! Auch je - ne Phan -

swum with - out de - lay To hear___ what he'll say. Fa - nat - i - cal

ta - sten, die im - mer - zu fa - sten: die Stock - fisch' ich mei - ne, zur___

cod___ who speak right to God,___ They fast in con - tri - tion With___

32

Pre - digt er schei - nen.
or-tho-dox con - vic - tion.

Kein_ Pre - digt nie-they_
No_ ser - mon they_

mal - len
all a - gree

den_ Stock - fisch so_ g'fal - len!
Has_ pleased them so_ swim-ming-ly. *(as if a parody)*

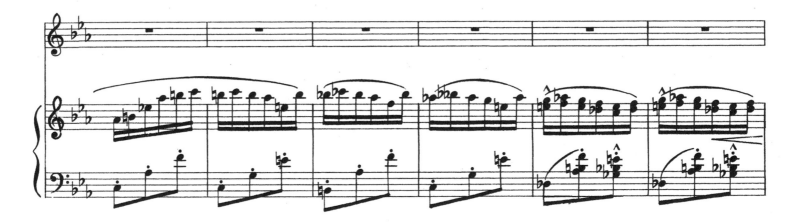

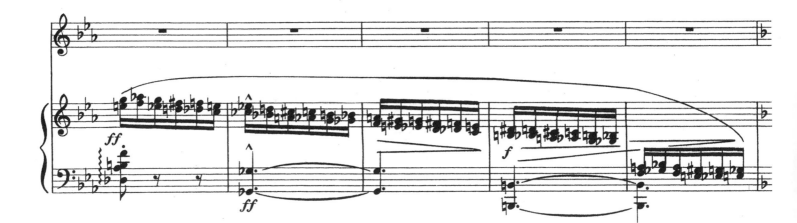

33

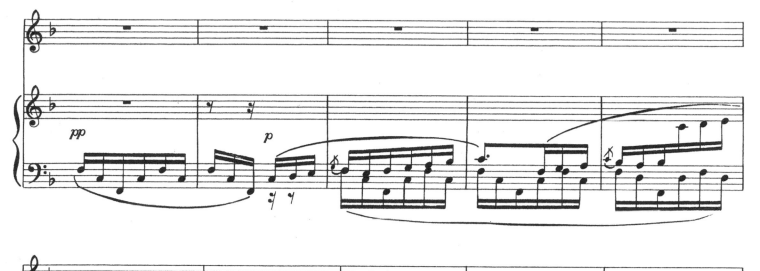

Gut
Plump

Aa - le und Hau - sen, die Vor - neh - me schmau - sen, die__ selbst sich be-
eels, snails, and_ oth - ers, Food for kings and their broth - ers, To__ hear this fine

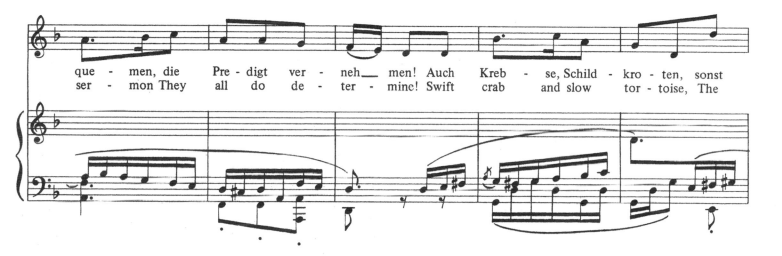

que - men, die Pre - digt ver - neh__ men! Auch Kreb - se, Schild - kro - ten, sonst
ser - mon They all do de - ter - mine! Swift crab and slow tor - toise, The

(cantabile)

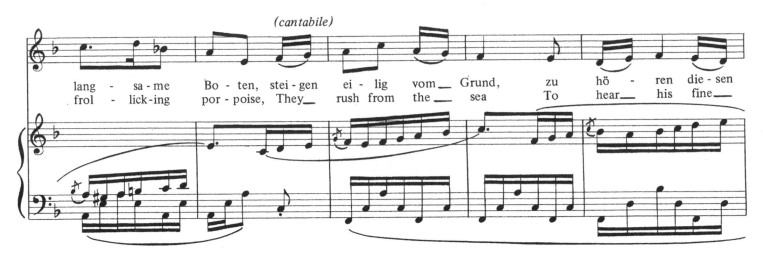

lang - sa - me Bo - ten, stei - gen ei - lig vom Grund, zu hö - ren die - sen
frol - lick - ing por - poise, They rush from the sea To hear his fine

Mund! Kein Pre - digt nie - mal - len
plea! No ser - mon they all agree

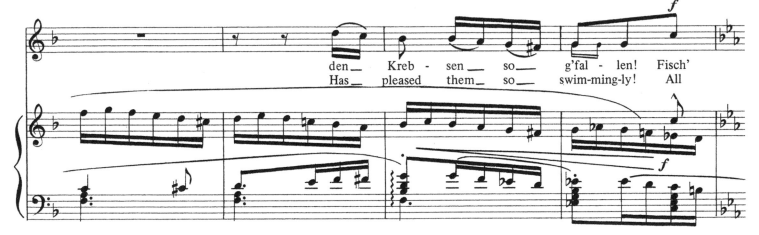

den Kreb - sen so g'fal - len! Fisch'
Has pleased them so swim - ming - ly! All

gros - se, Fisch' klei - ne, vor - nehm' und ge - mei - ne, er - he - ben die
fish large or small - er, Of rank low or tall - er, They come in pro -

Köp - fe wie ver-ständ' - ge Ge - schöp - fe.
fu - sion And__ know no con - fu - sion.

And__
They__

Got - tes Be - geh - ren
o - bey God's__ wish - es

die__ Pre - digt an-
Like o - be - di - ent lit-tle

hö - ren!
fish - es!

(with humor)

stacc.

Die Pre - digt ge - en - det ein Je - der sich
The ser - mon is fin-ish-ing, The au - di - ence

wen - det! Die
di-min-ish -ing. The

Hech - te_ blei - ben Die - be, die Aa - le_ viel lie - ben; die_ Pre - digt hat_
pike steals_ his_ din - ner, The eel's still a_ sin - ner, The_ words were de -

g'fal - len, sie blei - ben_ wie Al - len! Die_ Krebs' geh'n zu rük - ke, die_
light - ful, But_ na - ture's_ still spite - ful! Crabs_ back - ward of ne - ces-si - ty, Cods_

Stock-fisch bleib'n dik - ke, die_ Karp - fen viel_ fres - sen, die_ Pre - digt ver -
sin - ful o - be - si - ty, The_ carp is still_ pig - gish, The_ saint now seems_

ges - sen, ver - ges - sen! Die_ Pre - digt hat g'fal - len, sie_
prig - gish, seems_ prig - gish! His_ ser - mon was_ clev - er But_

blei - ben wie_ Al - len! Die Pre - digt hat g'fal - len, hat
fish are fish for ev - er, Die for ev - er, hat for

g'fal - len!
ev - er!

Strong Imagination
(Starke Einbildungskraft)

from *Lieder und Gesange
aus der Jugenzeit (1882)*
English paraphrase by B.M.

Gustav Mahler

I Love Love
(J'aime L'amour)

Louis Gallet - Eugene Oudin

Georges Bizet

Tu veux sa-
You want to

voir_____ si je pré - fè - re_____ La mau - res - que aux yeux lan - guis -
know_____ if I pre - fer_____ The Moor-ish maid - en's drow - sy

sants,___ Ou bien la juive_____ au front sé - vè - re, Ou la
eye,___ Or else the A - sian proud, or her,_____ the Greek with

41

grecque, iv - res - se des sens? Dans mon coeur, fo - yer___ plein de
beau - ty from on___ high? In my heart now full___ of

cen - dre,___ Tout___ est gla - cé, je le sens bien.___ Mon
ash - es gray,___ All___ now is ice, I know it well.___ My

sou - ve - nir y peut des - cendre Hé - las! il n'y ral - lu - me
thoughts in vain may surge but nay! No sparks a - mong the ash- es

rien, il n'y ral - lu - me rien. Hé -
dwell, a - mong the ash - es dwell. A -

43

mour,   l'a mour,   l'a - mour,   l'a-mour,   l'a - mour,   Ah!____
lone,   for love,   a - lone!   for love   a - lone,   Ah____

____ j'ai - me l'a - mour,____ ____   oui ____ j'ai - me l'a -
____ for love a lone,____   for ____ love ____ I

mour!   Dans la
live.   With -

cou - pe ____ qu'el - le ca - res - se   Ma lèvre en feu n'a qu'un tré -
in the cup my lips ca - ress,____   One prize a - lone my eyes can

sor; ___ Le vin qui nous ver - se l'iv - res - se Dans l'ar -
see; ___ The wine that __ spar - kles none the less ___ Though

gi - le ___ com - me dans l'or. Pour - vu qu'il ait la mê - me
gold or lead the cup may be. If ___ but the wine has the same

flam - me, ___ Le mé - tal peut chan - ger ___ cent fois, ___ Si
fire ___ The __ met - al may be that ___ or this, ___ If

l'a - mour par - fu - me mon â - me, Qu'im - por - te la
love but bear my spir - it high - er, What care I ___

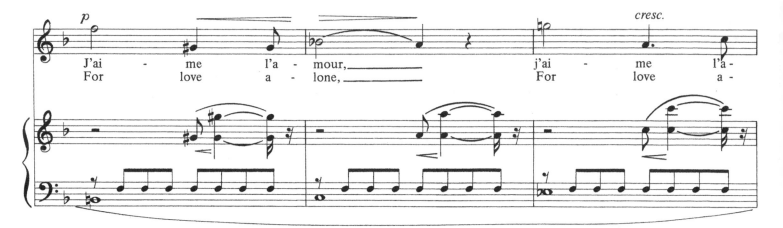

J'ai - me l'a - mour,_____ j'ai - me l'a-
For love a - lone,_____ For love a -

mour, l'a - mour, l'a - mour, l'a - mour, l'a - mour, Ah!_____
lone, for love a - lone, for love a - lone, Ah,_____

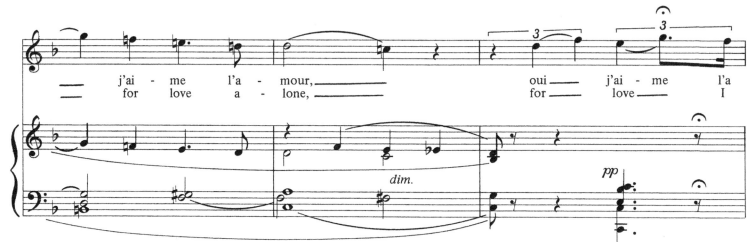

____ j'ai - me l'a - mour,_____ oui___ j'ai - me l'a
____ for love a - lone,_____ for___ love___ I

mour!
live!

to Mademoiselle Jeanne Granier

Ballad of the Fat Turkeys
(Ballade des Gros Dindons)

Edmond Rostand
English text by B.M.

Emmanuel Chabrier

vant la pas - tou - re qui fi - le,
front of their slow strol - ling shep - herd

En fre - don - nant de vieux fre - dons, Vont en
Who whis - tles old ___ mel - o - dies ___ Come

pro - ces - si - on do - ci - le Les gros din -
in do - cile pro - ces - sion, The fat tur -

Mouvt. de Valse

dons!
keys!

p e con grazia

ment te - nir un con - ci - le, Les gros din -
sol - emn - ly hold their coun - cil, The fat tur -

dons.
keys.

N'a - yant ja - mais trou - vé tou-chants Les sons que le ros - si - gnol
They've nev - er lived in fan - ta - sy, The world of the night - in - gale's

file, Ils sui - vent lourds et tré - bu - chants, L'un d'eux dig - ne comme un é-
songs.___ They strut a - bout so clum - si - ly With the dig - ni - ty high of-

di - le ; Et lor - squ'au loin - tain cam - pa - ni - le L'an - gé - lus fait ses
fice brings And when from the dis - tant bell tow - er The an - ge - lus sounds

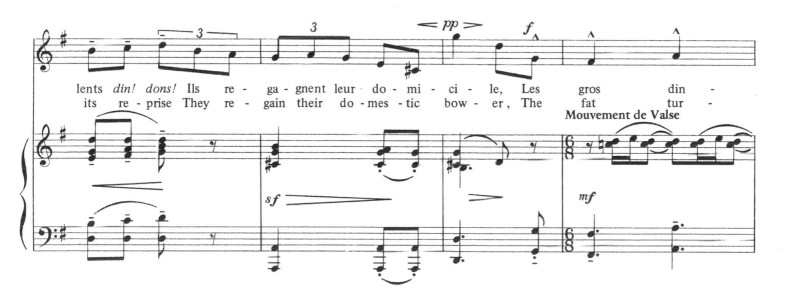

lents *din! dons!* Ils re - ga - gnent leur do - mi - ci - le, Les gros din -
its re - prise They re - gain their do - mes - tic bow - er, The fat tur -

Mouvement de Valse

52

Prud'hommes gras, leurs seuls penchants Sont vers le pratique et l'u
Men of affairs, their sole desire Is for the mundane and the

ti - le, Pour eux, l'a - mour et les doux chants Sont un pas - se - temps trop fuu - tile, For them sweet songs of hearts a - fire___ Are pas - times much too

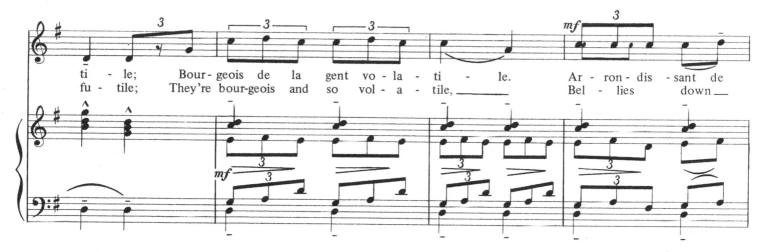

ti - le; Bour-geois de la gent vo - la - ti - le. Ar - ron-dis - sant de
fu - tile; They're bour-geois and so vol - a - tile, ___ Bel - lies down ___

noirs be - dons, Ils se fi - chent de toute i - dyl - le, Les gros din -
to their knees, they dis - dain an - y sweet i - dyl, ___ The fat tur -

dons.
keys.

to Mademoiselle Mily-Meyer

Villanelle of the Little Ducks
(Villanelle des Petits Canards)

Rosemonde Gerard
English text by B.M.

Emmanuel Chabrier

vont, / come, les pe - tits ca - nards, / the __ lit - tle ducks, Tout au bord de la ri - vie - re, / All a - long the riv - er banks

Com - me de bons cam - pa - gnards. __ / Like gay young coun - try __ bucks. __

55

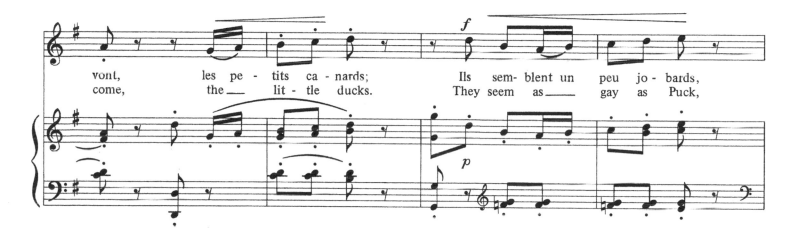

Barboteurs et frétillards. Heureux de troubler l'eau claire, Ils
Paddlers who run amok Disturbing the clear water They

vont, les petits canards; Ils semblent un peu jobards,
come, the little ducks. They seem as gay as Puck,

Mais ils sont à leur affaire, Comme de bons campagnards!
But each is minding his affair Like a gay young country buck.

Dans l'eau pleine de têtards, Où
In water where the tadpole sucks, And

56

tremble une her - be lé - gè - re, Ils vont, les pe - tits ca - nards, Mar - chant par
where a light grass trem - bles, They come, the __ lit - tle ducks, March - ing

grou - pes é - pars, D'une al - lu - re ré - gu - liè - re, Com - me de bons cam pa gnards.__
nip and __ tuck, With clock-work reg - u - lar - i - ty, Like gay young coun - try bucks.__

Dans le beau vert d'é - pi - nards De l'hu - mi - de cres - son -
Where the far - mer spin - ach plucks, From the wa - ter cres - s's

niè - re, Ils vont, les pe - tits ca - nards, Et quoi qu'un peu go - gue - nards,
bed, __ They come, the __ lit - tle ducks, And though a quar - rel's struck,

Ils sont d'hu - meur dé - bon - nai - re, Com - me de bons cam - pag - nards!
They seem to be so deb - on - air, Like a young coun - try___ buck.___

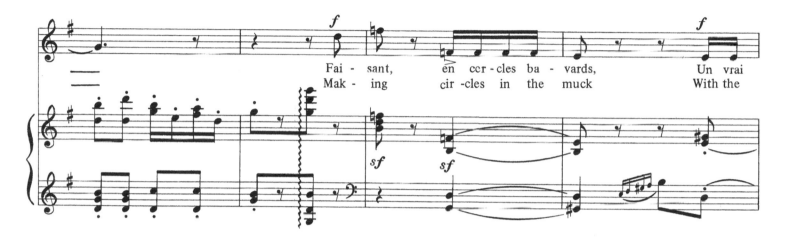

Fai - sant, en cer - cles ba - vards, Un vrai
Mak - ing cir - cles in the muck With the

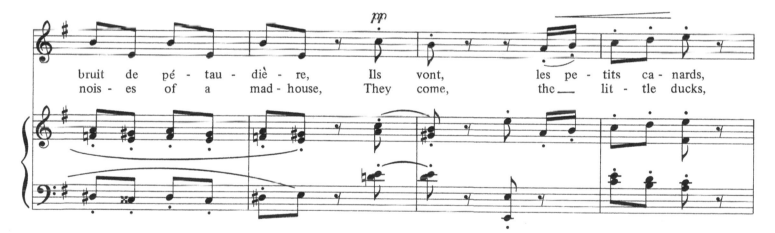

bruit de pé - tau - diè - re, Ils vont, les pe - tits ca - nards,
nois - es of a mad - house, They come, the___ lit - tle ducks,

Do - dus, lus - tres et gail - lards, Ils sont gais à leur ma - niè - re,
Chub - by, and full of___ pluck, They are gay in their own way,

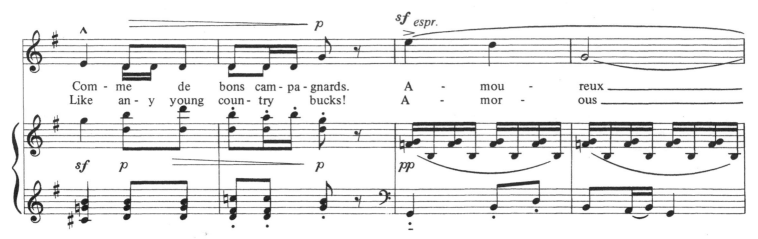

Com - me de bons cam-pa-gnards. A - mou - reux ____
Like an - y young coun-try bucks! A - mor - ous ____

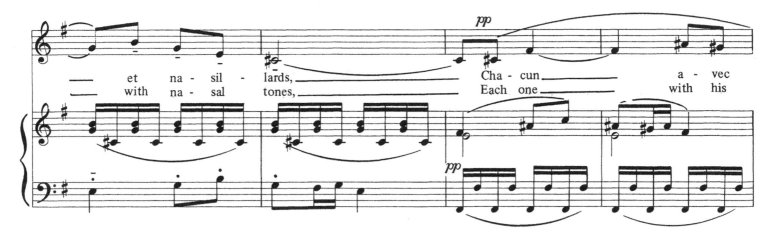

____ et na - sil - lards, ____ Cha - cun ____ a - vec
____ with na - sal tones, ____ Each one ____ with his

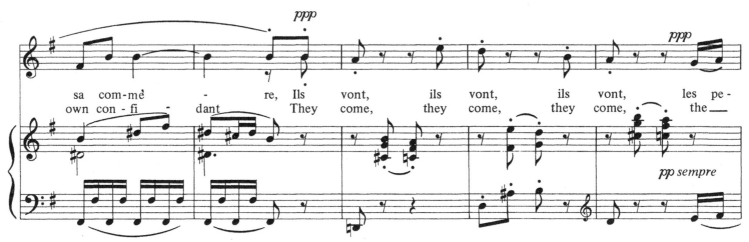

sa com-mè - re, Ils vont, ils vont, ils vont, les pe-
own con-fi - dant They come, they come, they come, the ____

tits ca - nards, Com - me de bons cam - pa - gnards.
lit - tle ducks, Like gay young coun - try ____ bucks.

The Classicist
(Klassik)

English paraphrase by B.M.

Words and Music by
Modeste Mussorgsky

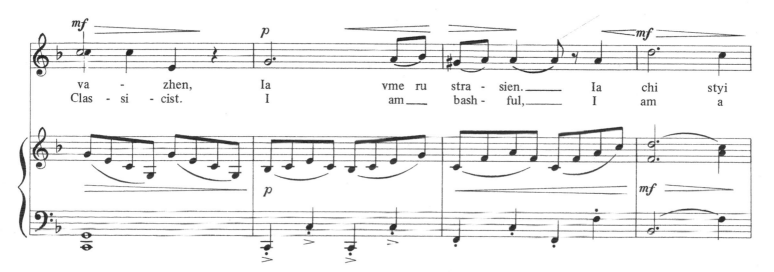

60

Klas - sik, Ia styd liv,___ Ia chi styi klas - sik,___ Ia___ uch
Clas - si - cist, Ver - y po - lite, my pas - sions are___ al - ways___ quite___ con -

(Vigorously)

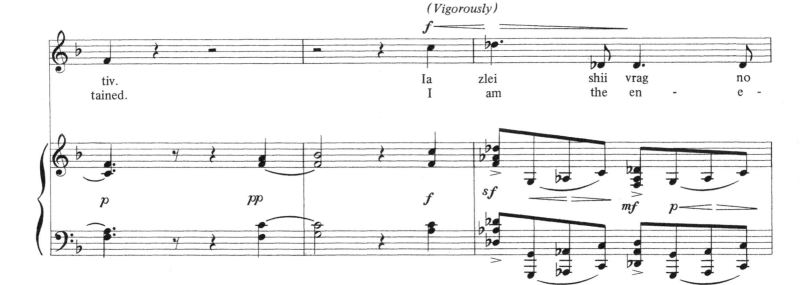

tiv. Ia zlei shii vrag no
tained. I am the en - e -

vei shikh u - khishch re - nii, za klia tyi vrag
my of all that's mod - ern, All in - no - va -

vsekh .... no vo vve de nii. .... Ikh
tions .... bring me close to tears. .... Their

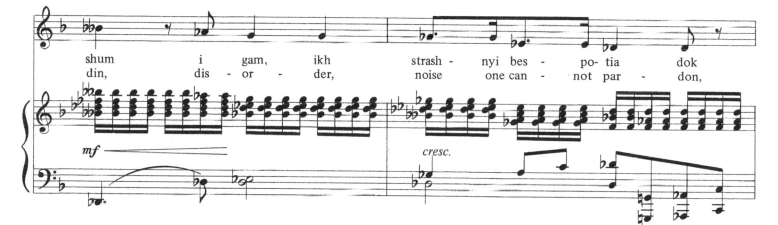

shum i gam, ikh strash - nyi bes - po - tia dok
din, dis - or - der, noise one can - not par - don,

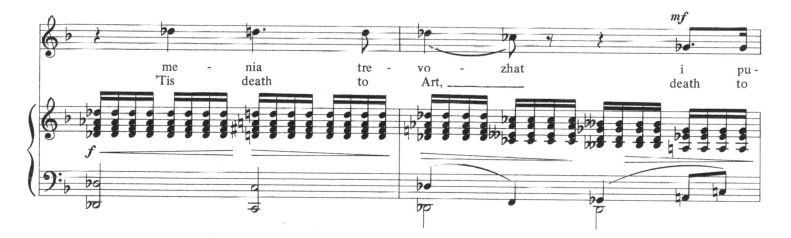

me - nia tre - vo - zhat i pu -
'Tis death to Art, _____ death to

ga - iut.
Art. _____ V nikh grob is - kus stva vizhu
The re - al - iz - ation of my

Ia. No Ia, Ia prost, no Ia, Ia Ia - sen, Ia
fears. But I am plain, pre - cise, po - lite_____ and

skro - men, vezh - liv, Ia_____ pre kra - sen. Ia chi styi klas - sik,
wonder-ful, grace - ful, flow - ing, re-strained, The pur-est Clas-si - cist,

Ia styd liv._____ Ia chi styik las_____ sik, Ia_____ uch - tiv.
Ver - y po - lite, My pas- sions are__ al - ways quite_____ con - tained.

The Seminarist
(Seminarist)

English paraphrase by B.M.

Words and Music by
Modeste Mussorgsky

Allegro moderato

Pa - nis, pis - cis, cri - nis, fi - nis, ig - nis, la - pis, pul - vis, ci - nis, Ach tyi
Oh! Oh!

go - re moye go - re Or - bis, am - nis et ca - na - lis,
Woe is me, Oh woe is me!

or - bis, am - nis et ca - na - lis. Vot tak za - dal pohp mne tas - koo
See the blow that Fa - ther Sim - yon gave me.

za za - gri vok da poh she - yeh on bla - goh - slo
Such a bles - sing on my head from his ho - ly hand I can hard - ly

64

vil stand,
ee des - ni - tseh yu svya - toh - yu pah mya - ti - li-
Such a bles - sing on my head from his ho - ly hand I can - not

shil stand.
Fas - cis, a - xis, fu - nis, en - sis,

fus - tis, vec - tis ver - mis men - sis. Ooh poh - pa Sye - myo - na dotch - ka Znat - na - ya ta -
Fa - ther Sim - yon has a daugh - ter, Blush - ing cheeks ro - ses

ka - ya. Shtotch - ki, tchto tvoy ma - kov tsvet, glaz - ki - s poh - voh -
mock. Lan - guid eyes that glow with laugh - ter, Bo - som swel - ling

lo - koy; *grood leh - bya zha - ya, da poh - ka - ta - ya, pohd roo - bah - shetch - koy
neath her smock. Fa - ther Sim - yon's daugh - ter, Fa - ther Sim - yon's daugh - ter, lan - guid eyes, Blush - ing

vskoh - likh - noo - lah - sya Fa - cis, a - xis, fu - nis, en - sis, fus - tis, ves - tis, ver - mis, men - sis...
cheeks of red, bos - om...

Ach - tih, Styo - sha, moh - ya Styo - sha tak tye - byah rahs - tseh - loh -
Son - ya, Son - ya, my love, I want to clasp you to my ach - ing

vahl Bih, krehp - koh, nah - krehp - koh K serd - tsoo pri -
breast, And hold you close un - til my pas - sion is

* Soft sound.

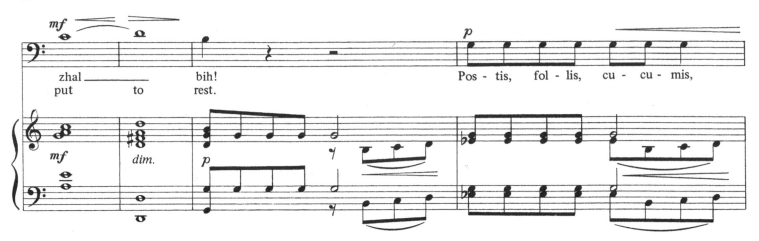

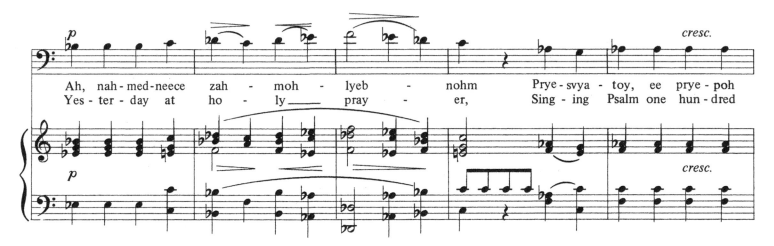

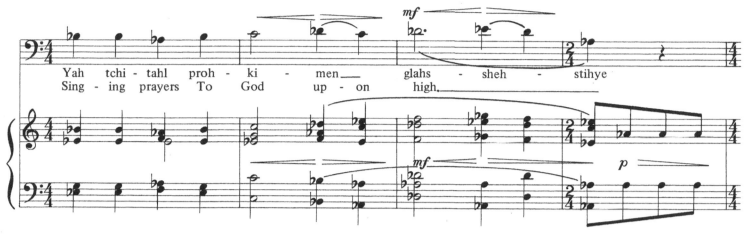

Yah tchi-tahl proh- ki- men___ glahs -sheh -stihye
Sing- ing prayers To God up- on high.___

Ah nah Styo- shoo leh- vihm glah- zahm vsyo poh- smah- tree___ vahl,___ ah nah
Then the love -ly___ Son - ya, Son - ya, Then the love- ly Son - ya hap - pened by, Oh,

leh - viye klee - ros vsyc zah - glya - dih - vahl,___ da pohd- mahr - gih - vahl.___
Son - ya, Son - ya, Then the love- ly Son - ya caught my eye, Oh love- ly___ Son - ya.

Tchor - tohv
Just then

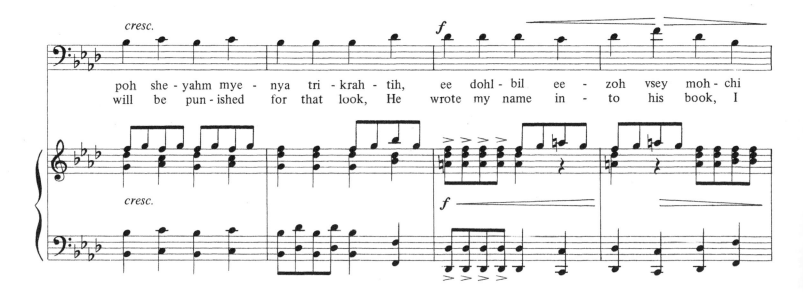

mnye v'bash - koo lah - tihñ oo kahz - koy. Or - bis, am - nis et ca - na - lis,
will be pun - ished for that look.

et ca - na - lis, san - guis, un - guis et an - na - lis, et an - na - lis.

Tak oht bye - sah - ees - koo -
That's how Sa - tan temp - ted me

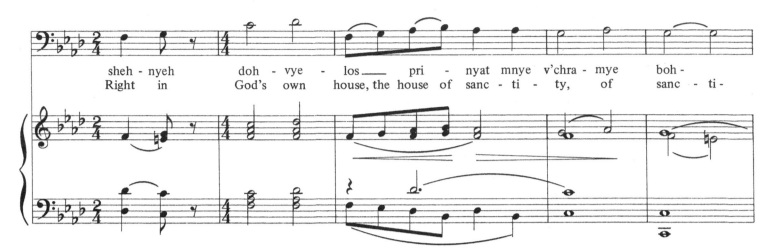

sheh - nyeh doh - vye - los___ pri - nyat mnye v'chra - mye boh -
Right in God's own house, the house of sanc - ti - ty, of sanc - ti -

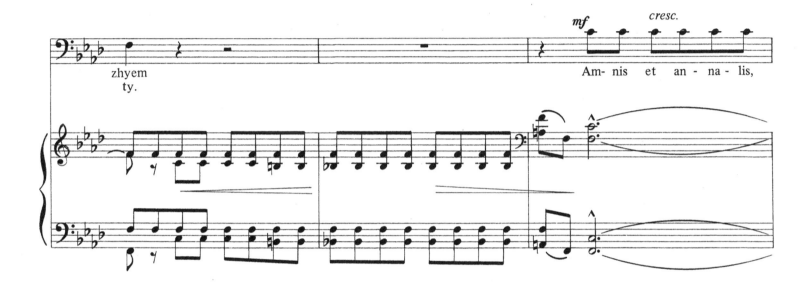

zhyem
ty.

Am - nis et an - na - lis,

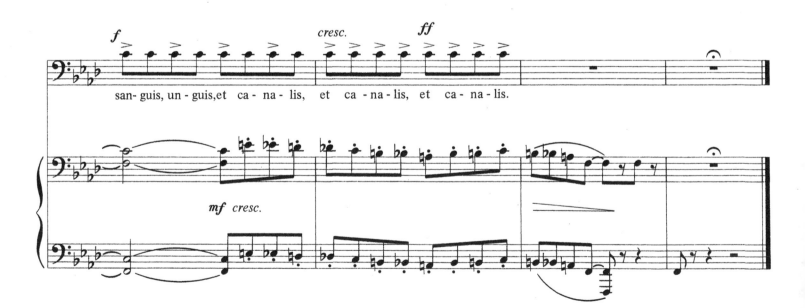

san - guis, un - guis, et ca - na - lis, et ca - na - lis, et ca - na - lis.

If You've Only Got A Moustache

George Cooper

Stephen C. Foster

1.Oh! all of you poor sin - gle men,___ Don't ev - er give up in de - spair, For there's al - ways a chance while there's

tache, If you've on - ly got a mous - tache. _____

2.
No matter for manners or style,
No matter for birth or for fame,
All these *used* to have something to do
With young ladies changing their name,
There's no reason now to despond,
Or go and do any thing rash,
For you'll do though you can't raise a cent,
If you'll only raise a moustache!
A moustache, a moustache,
If you'll only raise a moustache.

3.
Your head may be thick as a block,
And empty as any foot-ball,
Oh! your eyes may be green as the grass
Your heart just as hard as a wall.
Yet take the advice that I give,
You'll soon gain affection and cash,
And will be all the rage with the girls,
If you'll only get a moustache,
A moustache, a moustache,
If you'll only get a moustache.

4.
I once was in sorrow and tears
Because I was jilted you know,
So right down to the river I ran
To quickly dispose of my woe,
A good friend he gave me advice
And timely prevented the splash,
Now at home I've a wife and ten heirs,
And all through a handsome moustache,
A moustache, a moustache,
And all through a handsome moustache.

My Wife Is A Most Knowing Woman

George Cooper

Stephen C. Foster

1. My wife is a most know-ing wom-an, She

al - ways is find-ing me out, She nev - er will hear ex - pla - na - tions But

in - stant - ly puts me to rout,_____ There's no use to try to de-

ceive her, If out with my friends, night or day,_____ In the most in - con - ceiv - a - ble

man - ner She tells where I've been right a - way,_____ She

says that I'm "mean and in - hu - man" Oh! my wife is a most know - ing wom - an.

2.
She would have been hung up for witchcraft
If she had lived sooner, I know,
There's no hiding any thing from her,
She knows what I do - where I go;
And if I come in after midnight
And say "I have been to the lodge,"
Oh, she says while she flies in a fury,
"Now don't think to play such a dodge!
It's all very fine, but wont do, man,"
Oh, my wife is a most knowing woman.

3.
Not often I go out to dinner
And come home a little "so so,"
I try to creep up through the hallway,
As still as a mouse, on tiptoe,
She's sure to be waiting up for me
And then comes a nice little scene,
"What, you tell me you're sober, you wretch you,
Now don't think that I am so green!
My life is quite worn out with you, man,"
Oh, my wi e is a most knowing woman!

4.
She knows *me* much better that I *do*,
Her eyes are like those of a lynx,
Though how she discovers my secrets
Is a riddle would puzzle a sphynx,
On fair days, when we go out walking,
If ladies look at me askance,
In the most harmless way, I assure you,
My wife gives me, oh! such a glance,
And says "all these insults you'll rue, man,"
Oh, my wife is a most knowing woman.

5.
Yes, I must give all of my friends up
If I would live happy and quiet;
One might as well be'neath a tombstone
As live in confusion and riot.
This life we all know is a short one,
While *some* tongues are long, heaven knows,
And a miserable life is a husband's,
Who numbers his wife with his foes,
I'll stay at home now like a true man,
For my wife is a most knowing woman.

The One Way
The True Philosophy of all Nice Conservatories of Music
and Nice "MUS DOC'S" "IMBCDGODAMILY"

Words and Music by
Charles E. Ives [1923?]

Here are things you've heard be - fore, Turned out dai - ly by the score, Pret - ty rhymes_ you know,_ How gent - ly on the ear They bring a smile or bring a tear, Do re mi fa mi re

[allegro, tempo di marcia]

do.

[mp- poco cresc.]

Nice Chorous

When we go a - march - ing Down thro' life and the Street, O

[mf]

loud and free must the mu - sic be With [the] tunes to match the

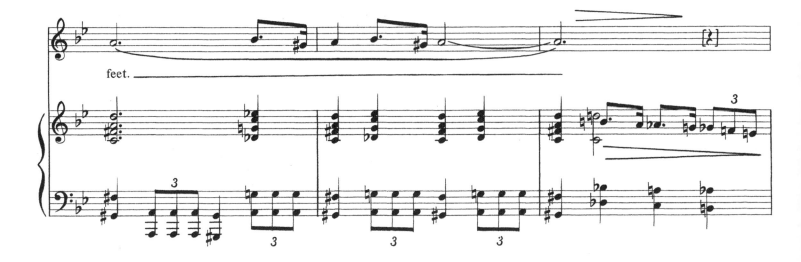

feet.

Now a soft-er ca - dence, Now we change___ the key,

Just to___ stage a come - back To the main strain___ of our___

glee. So___ if you'd go a - march - ing To For - tune or to___

Fame, Per - haps the saf - est way's to play the same_____ old,___ same_____ old___

game. Tunes we've of-ten heard be-fore, Snat-ches of a

[andante]

[mf dim. p]

doz-en more, Jin-gles row__ on row,_____ when borne up-on the ear, They

[poco]

bring a smile or bring a tear, Do re mi fa mi re

[non legato]

[poco]

do.____

[allegro, tempo di marcia]

[mp - poco cresc.]

When we go a - march - ing Down the aisle or the Street, O ____

nice and sweet must the mu - sic bleat, With [the] time to match the

feet. _____

Now a soft - er ca - dence, ____ Now we change ____ the key,

Just to ___ stage a come - back To the nice key ___ of our ___

glee.   So ___ if you'd go a - march - ing To For - tune or to ___

Fame,   The saf - est way's to play the same _____ old, same _____ old ___

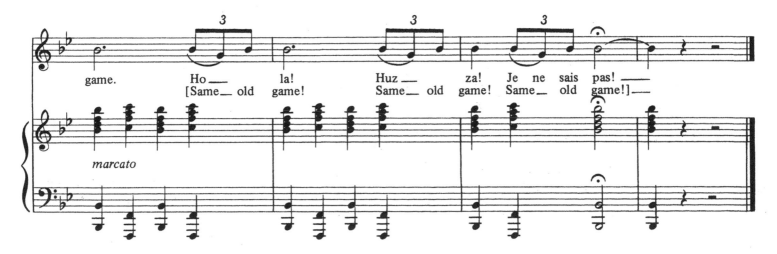

game.   Ho ___ la!   Huz ___ za! Je ne sais pas! ___
[Same ___ old game!   Same ___ old game! Same ___ old game!] ___

marcato

Promiscuity

from: Hermit Songs

9th Century*

Samuel Barber, Op. 29, No. 7

I do not know with whom E - dan**will sleep,

but I do know that fair E - dan will

not sleep a - lone.

*From Kenneth Jackson's *A Celtic Miscellany,* by permission of Routledge and Kegan Paul, Ltd., London, and Harvard University Press, Cambridge, MA.
**Edan: pronounce Ay - den.

Copyright, 1954, by G. Schirmer, Inc.

CHURCH BELL AT NIGHT

from: Hermit Songs

12th century
Translated by Howard Mumford Jones*

Samuel Barber, Op. 29, No. 2
Original key

Molto adagio ♩ = 46

Sweet lit - tle bell, struck on a wind - y night,

I would lie - fer keep tryst with thee Than be

With a light and fool - ish wo - man.

*From *Romanesque Lyric,* by permission of the University of North Carolina Press.

A Fine Line

Thomas Moore

Seymour Barab

luxury in it. So wheth-er we're on or we're

off, Some witch-er-y seems to a-wait you;_____ To

love you is pleas-ant e-nough_____ But

oh,_____ it's de-li-cious to hate you._____